HEART IN ASHES

UMER SHAH JEHAN

AURAQ

Printed in the Islamic Republic of Pakistan.
Printed: October, 2020
Edition: 1st
ISBN: 978-969-749-050-9
Price: Rs 1,000 PKR, $10 US

ISLAMABAD, PAKISTAN

raabta@auraqpublications.com.pk | +92-300-0571-530
www.auraqpublications.com.pk | @AuraqPublications
ISBN : 978-969-749-050-9

Book Cover designed by,

Abu Bakr Zafar - @psychowriter_

You lived
in my heart,
so I burnt
my heart
into ashes

just look
at my heart,
I have traces
of fire ashes
in my heart -
my heart has burnt
but the residue
of your memories
is still there

I saw my heart
burning
in the flames
of my love,
and I could not
save my heart
from dying.

how blissful
your heart must be
by seeing
my heart puffed,
my soul smoked,
and my love burning
to death.

my soul thought
that you are the warmth
that would soothe it,
but you were the fire
that burnt it instead.

My darling! don't find love
in the burnt walls
of my heart
you are just
looking for love
in a place
where love
was smoked
in a flicker
of flame.

My eyes don't cry
they bleed out,
because you were
flowing through
my blood
so I let you out
through my eyes.
I vacated my soul,
because you were
just flickering
my soul on fire.

Every time my heart
was unloved by someone
it loved,
I lost piece of my soul
they took away with them
my dead soul was alive
on this last part
that you took away

And the walls
of my room
are drenched
in pain -
they heard
my heart
breaking
into pieces
and the
aching
of my heart
has terrified them

take my hand
leave me
in the core
of fire
my soul
would be
burning,
but I would not
show a tinge
of burnt skin.

And yes
I am dry
my soul
is dry,
because
you sucked
all the love
that was coursing
in my veins

You did not
love me,
you just
chose me
when your heart
needed love,
and after
all my love
you just vanished -
what to do
with this void
in my heart now?

I kissed your scars
with all the love
I carried,
and your scars
got tired of
same love and lips
your scars craved
for new love and lips
to touch them

And I undressed
my soul,
and let the air
of love touch
my scars,
but even
the air of love
could not extinguish
the flames erupting
from my scars.

Each and every ounce
of my body misses you,
but stay as far as possible
I don't need you
to love you
I can love you
with broken pieces
of my love.

I fell for you
with the darkness
etched in my soul,
because you made
my scars less painful,
but in the end
it was you
who beat the
living shit out of me,
and flickered my scars
on fire.

bit by bit
my lovable,
and sassy heart
turned into
futile land
of emotions
all the love
I had for you
seeped away
through
the holes
of my heart.

I could have
spilled fire
on paper,
but my words
do not want to
touch you
like my heart did

And I have carved
my pain
on this paper
just touch it
with your hand,
and find yourself there

My heart
still dances
in the rain,
my fingers
still trace
your dancing
patterns,
my soul
still smells you
smiling in this rain

I am not
writing down
with words
tears just
spill down
on paper,
and they
shape into
poetry.

I could feel
your love
on your lips
when they
touched me
I wish
my scars
could feel
the love of
your lips too.

You were the moon
of my life,
but I could not
see you
in my bright days
my soul needed you
in bright light too.

I did so much
for you,
and still
I did not
even get
to say
a goodbye?

Someday
someone would
shake your soul
to the core,
and your heart
would call me
all at once.

I changed the pieces
of my soul
for you
even though
I hated the new pieces,
and now that you have left
how am I supposed
to love the pieces
of my soul
that I hate?

And if you
ever cross path
with me
ever again
just **don't** look
in my eyes
or else I would
fall for you again
or else I would
break for you again,
and you would
not be mine again.

My heart
was on its knees,
and it was begging
to let go the person
who was creating chaos
in the dark walls
of my heart.

I travelled
the lands
bare footed
for you,
but you
made me believed
that I chose
wrong destination.

I was like
a bottle
full of love,
but you did not
have the courage
to hold this bottle.

My heart sank
when my eyes saw
that strange world
of mine
falling onto lips
of someone else-

I did not knock
at your door
to beg
for your love
I knocked
to beg
for my heart
that I gave you.

She built herself
from the ashes
of my soul.

It was easy
to burn my heart
into ashes, right?
It was hell messy
to build a lovable heart
out of those ashes.

I don't want you back
in my life
to love you again,
but just place back
my heart
at its rightful place.

I let you go
for who you were
in the first place;
a visitor visiting
home of my heart.

I lost myself for a love
that never existed
I fell into a heart
that had its walls
painted with venom.

Each thought about you,
Each memory about us,
Each flashback about our love,
Each nostalgia of our romance
Is a step deeper
into grave of my heart.

The only thing
I did wrong was
that I did
all things right.

I was writing this book,
and you left in between
I wish you had stayed,
so that I could have written
happy end to this tragic story.

And look at my soul
try to climb in
jump into my soul
try to feel the pain
I gave you all I had
to make you whole -
you took pieces
of my soul.

I let you go
not because
I did not
love you
I let you go,
because you built
your home
in someone else
from the bricks
of my love.

You held my hand
in the sunshine,
but left me to suffer
in the dark
when I needed you
like my shadow.

I feel this fire
in my chest
that is turning
everything into ashes.

EVERY DAY
I LOSE A PART
OF MY SOUL

All you ever saw
was darkness,
because you did not
care to enter my heart
where I kept
all my light.

I held your hand
to climb every mountain
you held my hand
just to cross this bridge
where you did not see
any light
so you made me
your light.

You are the
hopeless picture
of breathing
but not living.

Sometimes,
I wonder
what made you
fall for me
If I was always
this kind of
heartless person
that you take me as.

I was destined
to doom,
for I handed you
the happiness
that used to
lit me up.

How can I say
that you are the one
when you cannot
even listen my silence,
and when your eyes
can't sense the
delusional shine
of my eyes.

I broke pieces
of my soul
in darkness
so that
no one could
gaze at the
sorrowful image
of you
that shines
in the pieces
of my soul.

I was on my way
to search your soul,
but I lost my own
in the process.

My eyes
are not
adaptive
to my heart.
they don't cry
when
my heart cries.

A part of my soul
loves you unconditionally,
and wants to give you
another chance,
but a part of my soul
wants to let you go
for letting me bleed,
and not even noticing

After turning me
into ashes,
after creating holes
in my soul
you are telling me
that I deserve better?
But what if that better
cannot fill my holes
that you have created forever?

I let a lot of people in,
and hold my hand
explore me
like never before,
but my heart
could not be saved.

I don't miss you
I miss myself
that used to exist
in the universe
of your eyes.

If you knew
how I used to
spend my nights
while you were away,
your heart would be
in ashes.

I have always loved
more than
I was ever loved
you told me
to sell pieces
of my heart
when you were meant
to gather the pieces
and make me whole.

I mourn
over the loss
of my heart
every day
these heavy beats
don't let me
breath
freely.

I will get over you
one day,
but what if
I don't want to
get over you ?
Because you dwell
in my soul,
and I cannot detach
my soul
from my body.

Stumbling in the dark,
and falling silently
and breaking
without any noise
is better
than holding
a rose
with thorn
forever.

I don't miss you
is what my eyes
would be telling you,
but
just put your hand
on my heart
I fuckin' need you
is what you would hear.

give me more pain
I would shape it
into poetry
hit me hard
break me
in tiny pieces
I would recollect
myself
and re-create myself
like a phoenix creates
itself
from its own ashes.

I was digging
into your soul
with each day passing by
I was falling
to love you
even harder
with each day
leaving behind,
but you were carrying
a heart
that was not yours
you were merely
carrying someone's heart
in your chest
how were you supposed
to feel my love?

I looked for you
in the places
where love
lived once,
but now
far gone.

She was a broken mess
I told myself
while gathering
the ashes
of my burnt heart.

You **don't** deserve her
If you **can't** be there for her
when is walking
on bricks and blades
you **don't** deserve her.
If you **can't** be there for her
when she is fighting
the demons alone in the dark
you **don't** deserve her.
If you **can't** be there for her
when she needs a shoulder
to lay her head on
you **don't** deserve her
If you **can't** be there for her
when she is losing her soul
in the deadliest of shadows.

I wondered that
why don't you smile
with me now
then I realized that
you may have
started to share
your wonderful smile
with someone else.

I drew you
on a piece
of white paper
but I forgot
to color you
that is what
you are -
a colorless
painting.

I wish
if you could
live forever
the way
my words
are living.

And I was
just another lover
with broken heart,
and dark words
that made her eternal
in the lines of poetry.

She died but
her love lived
in my heart
inside my soul
I kissed her love,
and let it live
for centuries

I was destined
to doom,
and then bloom
from the ashes
of my soul.

I told this frail heart
not to fall for you,
because you just
carried darkness,
but my heart
found peace
in your darkness.

Forge your heart
into a weapon
it must
not bleed.

Pain can hurt
Demons can haunt,
but love
my darling !
love can heal.

Let her
be wild,
and let
her enjoy
her wildness.

she was looking
for someone with who
she could be insane
and still be loved.

Take me back
to the night
when we parted
take me back
so that I can
mend my heart
with yours.

I let you go,
but be mindful
of the realization
that I taught you
how to love
So, my darling !
love harder
next time.

sometimes,
poets need
an inspiration,
to follow blindly,
a subject
to write poetry upon,
a painting
to lose into.
Thank you
for being the
painting
of my life.

Let me meet you
for one last time
let me make us eternal
by molding us
in the lines of poetry.

Diving into the lake
of your love
might be
my choice,
but drowning in it
and dying in it
was not.

It does not matter
where we left off things
I am still standing
at the same place
looking for the
same person.

And my tortured soul
was wandering
in search of shelter,
and then in a jiff
I landed in your heart,
and it felt like home -
your heart was my home.

And after standing
in the courtyard
of my heart
all I remember
is your love,
all I hear
is your voice.
the walls
of my heart
feels occupied
with your existence.

My heart was
a lonely wanderer
after being homeless
for a decade
after being high
on misery
after being taken over
by the footprints
of your love -
it found a home
in the ashes of your soul.

The way you smile
it tells a lot about
the dancing pattern
of your heart
the way you touch
it unravels the love
that your fingers crave for.

I wish
I could tell you
what effect
that mole
on your face
leaves on my heart -
I wish you had my eyes.

POETS ARE WARRIORS IN BATTLES UNKNOWN

It had always
been you
no other person
had ever excited
my heart
that much.

There was
something
in her
that other people
did not have
she looked
beautiful even
in her scars.

whiskey

in rain

led me

to you

I absorbed you
in my blood
the traces of which
run through
my body
and end up
in my heart.

You made me
fall for you
every single day
in million of ways.

I lost
a part of
myself
the day
my eyes
landed on
you.

I drank vine
like I drank
your soul
I am buzzed
with memories
like I was buzzed
with your love.

I aroused
from the ashes
of a heart
that knew
nothing,
but
love.

I lost you
on sand
of time,
and found you
when I smelled
my poetry books
in my bookshelf.

She wanted me
to write poetry
I, instead
made her poetry
that lived
in the heart
of lovers
for eternity.

And you were
a miracle
that cannot
be captured,
but only
lived.

And when I
planted a kiss
on your hands
it gave a re-birth
to my dying heart.

Holding your hands
into mine
gave me
most soulful touch
my heart ever tasted.

BILLION OF EYES ON YOU
AND YOUR HEART
MET MINE

I fell for you,
because of insanity
you had
when you touched me
in a way
sane people never did.

Your memories wander
in my heart,
and collide
with the walls
of my heart
like the clouds
on sky thunder,
and it begins
to rain.

I drunk
your
memories
like vine.

I just wanted
to be the poetry
that could be delivered
by your cozy lips.

Do not try
to seduce me
by your looks
the smile
you wore
on your lips
can do wonders.

I drunk the love
that you carried
in your eyes
the effects
of which are
etched
in my heart.

And I hope that
you would not
hold back when
I would show you
my scars
I hope that
you would
kiss my scars
the way
I kissed your soul.

Just hold
my hand
so tightly
that
it melts
my heart.

I would be yours
till my last breath,
because you taught me
to love
in the first place.

She collected tears
from my the blanket
of my eyes,
and put
my demons
at rest.

Tell her to take care of her, I would not be there for her. Tell her not to rust her heart with excruciating memories and hatred for me, all I ever wanted was love. Tell her to keep loving , keep living , keep falling , keep running , keep confronting but above of all keep breathing. Tell her to keep cherishing memories of me , tell her to remember me who made her learn to smile , who made her learn to laugh , who made her learn to fall for the right guy who can foresee her highs , her lows , her ecstasies , her cravings , her mood swings. Tell her to remember me as a man who bumped her into her heart where there was warmth of love, a man who bumped her into the depth and serenity of her eyes, who bumped her into the calmness of her soul that was worthy to be loved and cherished. Tell her I did everything I could to make her smile , tell her I did everything to quench the fire burning inside of her , tell her I did everything to save her from plunging into the stormy ocean of shadows , tell her I did everything to sparkle a ray of hope in her eyes and glimmering light inside of her. Tell her It was my shoulder who squeezed her tears and heard her darkest tales of gloominess, tell her it was my lap where she used to lay down her head where she needed peaceful sleep, tell her it was my hug that bore her wild sobbing every time she broke down, tell her it was my hug where she always found warmth and tranquility.

You never lost me completely. You lost me in pieces. Every time you un-loved me, you lost a piece of my soul on lands unknown, skies unexplored and oceans undiscovered. Every time I cried in front of you, and you just slept, like nothing happened - you lost me. When I had a bouquet in my hands for you, and you faked your smile, like it is not a big deal for you - you lost me. When you could not see the darkness behind my smile - you lost me. When you held my hand, but could not feel anything - you lost me. When you stopped sharing your cries with me - you lost me. When I used to play your favorite song, and your heart did not dance - you lost me. When there was rain in courtyard, and we stopped dancing in the rain – you lost me. When your smile could not toss my heart in joy - you lost me. When saying goodbye, instead of until then, became your habit - you lost me. When your lips started poisoning my lips - you lost me. When you used to sleep before I came back from work - you lost me. When my hand felt like a stranger's hand to you - you lost me. You lost me in ways unknown, in times uncountable.

You were never ready to fall in love with me, because to you, falling in love and falling apart were the same things. You were so focused on not falling in love, that you did not realize that falling in love could save you from falling apart. You were accustomed to be broken rather than letting someone in, and touching parts of your soul that no one touched. Everyone who came in your life, they just touched your body, not your soul. So, your heart just do not know what it is like to be loved. Your heart had not tasted love so it could not separate falling apart and falling for someone. Your heart fell apart every minute of every day because you never let vintage love touch your soul, you always let modern love touch your curves. Falling in love could have saved you from falling apart but you did not let your heart choose.

I wanted to make you a part of my soul. I craved you to explore the hidden ways of my heart in form of love, but you occupied space in my mind in the form of memories. You were stuck in the walls of my mind. You made me breakdown every single day. You made me a wreck and broken mess. You used to be in my heart for time eternity, now you are on my mind for how long I don't know. All I know is my mind can't get rid of you, and you are already there in my mental breakdowns but you are not with me because you are the reason of this broken mess in the first place.

And I wish you could visit my room, so that the walls of my room might show you the marks of pain etched on them when I used to break my soul in my own hands. The walls of my room were terrified and a horrendous fear had taken over them. They had witnessed me crying and shrieking and bleeding on my own broken pieces. They envied night, because they knew that they were going to tear down when my heart would call you in the dead of the night and you would not be there. My head leaning to the wall, my face in my hands, storm of tears rolling down my cheek, my heart sobbing heavily and my scars haunting me as bad as they could - my room envied it. I saw my blood on the walls, you painted the walls of my room with my blood.

I was not changing, I was breaking down. Every time, I tried to hold your hand, you just drew further apart. Every time, I asked you for a bit of light, you gave me handful of darkness. I was the damaged loner. I was standing at the edge of being falling apart, and I just wanted you to save me, but I forgot that it was you who pushed me to this edge, in the first place. I forgot that I was asking the person to make me whole who broke me into pieces, in the first place. I forgot that my soul was bleeding because you handed me this rose of love that had nothing but thorns. I forgot that i could not be saved by the person who scattered my pieces, in the first place.

I had to detach my soul from yours, because you were the pain in delight, and I was the blissfulness in chaos. I had to part my heart from yours because I was the glimmer of hope and you were the fall of a star. I had to turn away my eyes from your eyes because your eyes were occupied with existence of someone else, and my eyes were sacred enough not to fall for a heart that had been crowded with number of visitors. I had to part away because you were the scorching ray of sun, and I was serenity of moonlit night.

You left my soul, you vacated my heart, but the feelings I had for you, they are still there. I am still holding onto pain. My heart still aches of the pain that your feelings gave. You were my soul and I could not separate my soul from my body. I could not separate feelings from my heart, they are bound to be together. The walls of my heart are still painted with your love. My heart still bleeds the love that once was there but now dark cries. I still walk on the fire that flickers ashes in my heart. My heart still burns in these ashes. I am still burning in your far gone love and overlapping memories that hold my heart and soul.

My soul was lost and exhausted after the last scar that was left on the tainted walls of my soul. We never die all of a sudden, we die when someone leaves our soul with a piece of our soul, leaving behind a void, a scar in our soul. I had one last piece left in my soul, I was barely alive on that one piece, but you just took away that piece and flew away. After all the pieces of my soul were gone, my breathing had stopped and all the scars were haunting my hollow body with all the ache all the pain they had. My scars had put my heart on fire. I was burning in the ashes of my scars wilder than ever, and I would keep burning until someone finds me in the darkness and places a piece of their soul in the voids of my soul left by you. Till then, I would be a broken mess, a mess that is extinguished but still burning in the flames of his scars.

I was lost but I showed you the way to discover yourself. I was lost but I traded on pieces of my soul, so that you could breathe freely. I was in a dungeon of darkness with my hands chained to the wall, but my soul still lighting up your way with the little light I had left. I could have used that light to get out of this dungeon of darkness but I just could not see you stranded in darkness, you were a bird that was supposed to be wild, and to fly in open sky with all its wings feeling blissful. I let you have this light and explore the unexplored universe of yours. I was a mess destined to doom, but you were the lost-yet-beautiful mess that was not supposed to live in darkness for eternity. This dungeon was dark to the roots, and you were supposed to fly with the light you had.

When I stood in front of a mirror, I did not see myself, all I saw was you residing inside my soul, occupying my heart like a vacated house. But it scared the living shit out of me to see you flowing in blood. It hurt to see how your smile was painted in the insides of my soul. It hurt to see my heart crying and you smiling in my soul. My heart cried every damn day to stop beating. It grew tired of you making it difficult for it to beat. My demons were at large, taking over my damaged soul and untamed heart. I stopped looking in the mirror, because every time I saw myself in the mirror, I just saw you flowing in my veins like blood, and like blood, my heart refused to beat without you. You were just a piece of my soul, I could not detach from my soul.

I wish you could just read my eyes and hug me as tightly as possible. I wish the love in my heart could make its way into your heart, but your heart could not hear the magical melodies my heart wanted your heart to hear. I wish if you could penetrate deeper into my soul and see the scars that you flickered on fire. You were with me, but you were not with me. You could not sense the hurricane that was ripping up every thing inside of my soul. I was not changing, I was being consumed by the ashes of my heart and my soul was smoking in the air and you could not feel a single thing. It was my heart at fault, when it fell for you and thought that you can read it even when it did not want to be read.

I stopped feeling after you were gone. I denied every feeling, every sentiment. I could not cry. The love I had for you, stopped me from letting out a storm of tears. But then, I broke the mirror that used to be your favorite, ripped apart the books that smelled of your love, and let out a storm of tears, and with each tear, I let out your love from my soul. You were carved at the walls of my soul, with each tear that rolled down my cheek, I separated you from my soul. When I looked at the tears, they were miserable, because they carried my love for you and your love no more held control over my soul.

I could not purify my heart from ashes of your heart, even after everything the ashes were still there. Even after ending my soul, after jumping into an eternal force of death, I could not separate the ashes of your love. Death could kill my soul, but your love residing in me was an art that would live for centuries for modern lovers to witness what vintage love looks like. My love would be etched in the pages of poetry, that could not be ripped apart, that could only be read. It would ignite a pang of pain in the hearts that have ever loved someone. My death would not be in vain, it would pass the vintage love to the modern lovers. I would live for ever, my love would live forever.

My heart had stopped talking, but eyes, my eyes, they were talking out loud. My eyes were crying to be listened, my eyes just wanted to convey what my heart was bottling inside. But you could not read the eyes. My love was too real for you to understand. I had carried this love for way too long, it had started haunting my soul. My heart had given up for not being heard. A dancing heart learnt to be drown in silence. A lovable heart learnt to stop loving. Real love is too real for this generation to absorb. Their love come in gaps and pieces. They are far away from real love.

I let you be wild and I let you enjoy your madness. The sanely insane mess that you are with me, has my heart. I let you be mad and dance and toss in wilderness, it just multiplies my love for you. I freaking adore your insane soul rather than your sophisticated and decent soul. You are meant to do wonders with your wilderness. You are a perfect example of having chaotic angels and enjoy the every rain drop of this madness. My heart questions me every second that if not this chaotic angel, then who? My heart has rebelled that if not you, then no one. My heart has refused to fall for another soul when it just wants this chaotic angel that you are. I want to be mad with you, and be the epitome of wild love with you.

Nothing remains forever, not even love. But stay in my life for as long as you can, just love me as long as you can. Place your hand on my heart for as long as you can, be the music of my heart for as long as you can, hold me tightly in your hug for as long as you can, kiss me as hard as you can, taste my lips as better as you can. Dive into my eyes as deep as you can, cuddle with me for as many mornings as you can, sip as many coffees with me as you can, count the stars with me for as long as you can. Rest on my shoulder for as long as you can, sleep on my lap for as long as you want, watch movies with me for as long as you can, dance with me for as long as you can. Before tragedy rips us apart, I just want every bit of your heart and soul to be mine, I just want to feel you breathing in my soul.

I swum every ocean for you, because you matter in a way no one ever did. You are worth falling. You are worth breaking my heart for. You are worth falling off this climb of love. You are worth the risk. You attract my heart with this musical melody of your dancing heart. You hold the strings of my heart. The way you smile, it triggers something inside my heart. I feel lost in the moment, as if clocks have stop moving, day and night have been stuck, water has been still in oceans. You are the magic that happens once in a while, and has happened to me.

I found a piece of my soul in yours, because there was light in your soul with which you had bloomed my soul. You entered the room of my heart without knocking, but I didn't envy you entering this dark room, because you just entered and your light had lit the entire place of my heart. Now I can see the beauty of my heart in the light that you brought with you. You made me believe how much lovable I am. You made me believe how worthy I am. You gave me butterflies in my stomach. I feel more alive because I can feel you breathing in the room of my heart. My existence was incomplete, you completed me.

And a dinner date is not kind of date I want. I just want a rain-date with you. There would be heavy rain, and I would be dancing with you in the rain. I would be wearing black, and you would melting my heart in red. Your hand would be in mine, and we would be dancing and letting the rain touch our hearts like the love touched. After having dance with you, I would be on one knee, and I would be making you mine for ever, and the rain would be smiling at us and getting jealous of my love for you. We would get wet in the rain of love and you would be mine. The kind of date that would live for centuries, the kind of date I want with you.

I fell in love with you when I did not know what love is. It was you who told me how to fly on clouds of happiness without flying. It was you who told me that sometimes, people just hold your hand and never leave it in between. It was you with who my heart could dance and sing this rhyming song of love. It was you, who held the pieces of soul in the most perfect manner. I could find myself in your heart; the most beautiful place I have ever seen. I never believed why people fall in love but as soon as my eyes fell on you, love made sense. The structure of my heart altered the moment I saw you. You were the wonder that my heart was waiting to explore.

Again and again, I was told that happiness comes from inside you. And if happiness comes from inside, then you are my happiness, because you are inside me, inside me heart. There are traces of your love in the walls of my heart. I looked every where for happiness, but it is my heart where my happiness resides, where you reside. I have touched this happiness now. I have smelled this scent now. I have overlapped this happiness over my heart and soul and it would always glow my soul, you would always glow my soul with the magic you have.

With you, it does not feel that I am risking my heart. It just feels that I am putting the pieces of my heart in their rightful order. My heart just feels like breathing, it just feels like loving, it just feels like living, it just feels like itself. I am living through your heart. You have made me more alive. You came like magic, and you revived my dying heart. With you, it all feels so perfect. My heart feels lovable, when it is with you. It is ready to fall, it is ready to risk itself, because you are worth the risk. It knows that you would not let it break, you would be there for it. You are the love that my heart craved for so much. You are light that my dark heart wanted to enter into for so long.

I just want to be the art on the canvas of your heart. I just want to be the art; the forgotten one. I want you to paint me with the brushes of your eyes, and color me with the love you have in your heart. I want to be the eternal art hanging on the walls of your heart. I want to be the kind of art that you can not erase, not now, not ever. I want to be the epitome of eternal love. I want the modern lovers to look upon this canvas and wish to have this kind of love that I have for you. Even our hearts would faint with time, but the art that you would create with your love, it would live forever in every heart that wants to love and to be loved.

Stay with me no matter how weird I am. Stay with me, my hard side wants you to soothe me in ways only you know. The way you soothe my demons every night, before they haunt me, I adore that. Just stay as long as you can, I can not look into the eyes of these demons alone. Just hold my hand, I want to feel the feeling of what it is like to be loved and never un-loved after that. Just look into my eyes and don't look away after that, you soothe me in ways even you don't know.

Just sit in front of me. Let me fill my canvas with the art that you are. My brushes want to touch the canvas and define the phenomenal art that you are. Art drips from every inch of your existence. You are the art that poets portray in their poetry. You are the kind of art that lives forever. You are the art that starts with beauty and never ends. You dwell in the hearts of those who wear beauty in their hearts. You are the kind of art my brushes crave to draw on canvas. My brushes feel loved to touch the canvas to make you eternal.

You dwelled in my heart unannounced; a place where my poetry resided. So, I turned you into poetry, I made you something that has kept me alive so far. You were the kind of poetry that was missing from blood, I let you flow in my veins and I let you flow in every part of my soul. I let you touch every part of my soul. I etched you in my poetry books. I let you live in my room, in my bookshelf for ever and ever. The scent of your presence in my room made me love you even more. Your presence in my room let you dive into your soul even more.

Every day, my soul grabs you more tightly. Every day, I want to love you even more. The smile that you wear on your lips, it pushes me to love you harder everyday. The way you blink your eyes with innocence, it just melts my heart. The way you roll your lips in amazement, it just curls my stomach. The way you close your eyes and take your face in your hands, it just makes my heart beat fast. I love you in different way everyday, I fall for you in different way everyday.

When I wake up, I just want to land my eyes on you. I just want to see what miracle looks like. I want to take off this disappointment that I am wearing on my eyes, I just want to capture you in the roll of my mind. I want to save your essence in my soul for ever. I want your scent to bloom my soul till my last breath. You are the miracle I was waiting for centuries. You make me whole.

Before loving you, I lived you. I lived through your heart. I lived in your soul. I adore the broken mess that you are. I adore you to the whole. The way you deliver words, they sound like drunk from the love that you hid in your soul. I adore you to the whole. I adore you from one possible point to another possible point. I adore you when you make me feel jealous so that you could feel the love in my jealousy. I adore you when you crave to get attention. I adore you when you make efforts to talk to me even when I feel like disappearing in my darkness. I adore you the way you hold my hand when my head feels like a messy place. Your mere touch drives away all the heaviness. I adore you, I live in you, and every ounce of my soul feels in love with you. I love you to the whole.